AWESOME DOGS

Chihuahuas

by Mari Schuh

BELLWETHER MEDIA · MINNEAPOLIS, MN

Note to Librarians, Teachers, and Parents:

Blastoff! Readers are carefully developed by literacy experts and combine standards-based content with developmentally appropriate text.

Level 1 provides the most support through repetition of high-frequency words, light text, predictable sentence patterns, and strong visual support.

Level 2 offers early readers a bit more challenge through varied simple sentences, increased text load, and less repetition of high-frequency words.

Level 3 advances early-fluent readers toward fluency through increased text and concept load, less reliance on visuals, longer sentences, and more literary language.

Level 4 builds reading stamina by providing more text per page, increased use of punctuation, greater variation in sentence patterns, and increasingly challenging vocabulary.

Level 5 encourages children to move from "learning to read" to "reading to learn" by providing even more text, varied writing styles, and less familiar topics.

Whichever book is right for your reader, Blastoff! Readers are the perfect books to build confidence and encourage a love of reading that will last a lifetime!

This edition first published in 2016 by Bellwether Media, Inc.

No part of this publication may be reproduced in whole or in part without written permission of the publisher. For information regarding permission, write to Bellwether Media, Inc., Attention: Permissions Department, 5357 Penn Avenue South, Minneapolis, MN 55419.

Library of Congress Cataloging-in-Publication Data
Schuh, Mari C., 1975- author.
  Chihuahuas / by Mari Schuh.
    pages cm. – (Blastoff! Readers. Awesome Dogs)
  Summary: "Relevant images match informative text in this introduction to Chihuahuas. Intended for students in kindergarten through third grade"–Provided by publisher.
  Audience: Ages 5-8.
  Audience: K to grade 3.
  Includes bibliographical references and index.
  ISBN 978-1-62617-305-7 (hardcover : alk. paper)
  1. Chihuahua (Dog breed)–Juvenile literature. 2. Dogs–Juvenile literature. I. Title. II. Series: Blastoff! Readers. 2, Awesome Dogs.
  SF429.C45S38 2016
  636.76-dc23
                                    2015034836

Printed in the United States of America, North Mankato, MN.

Table of Contents

What Are Chihuahuas?

Chihuahuas are one of the smallest dog **breeds** in the world.

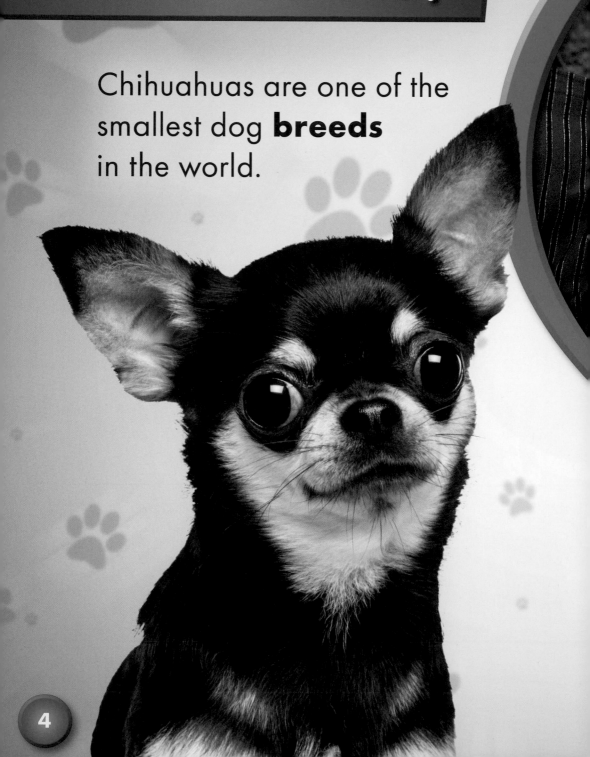

These charming dogs are
popular pets. They are smart
and **alert**.

Chihuahua Profile

large, upright ears —

lean body

— thin legs

Life Span: 15 to 17 years

Trainability:

(1) (2) (3) (4) (5) (6)

Hardest to train   Easiest to train

Chihuahuas have **lean** bodies
and thin legs.

Their large ears stand up.
Chihuahuas have big,
round eyes.

Chihuahuas weigh
6 pounds (3 kilograms)
or less.

Their small size puts them in the **Toy Group** of the **American Kennel Club**.

Most Chihuahuas have short **coats**. Their hair is smooth and **glossy**.

Others have long, soft coats.
Hair can be straight or wavy.

This breed often has chocolate, black, **fawn**, or red fur.

Chihuahua Coats

chocolate   black   fawn

red

The dogs can have markings on their coats. Some have patches of white fur.

Chihuahuas may have come from little dogs called **Techichis**.

Techichis lived in Mexico more than 1,000 years ago.

Mexico

N
W E
S

Chihuahua

N
W E
S

Chihuahuas were named
after a Mexican state,
Chihuahua. The dogs
came to the United
States around 1850.

The dogs soon became popular pets in the United States.

Loyal and Sassy

Today, Chihuahuas are **loyal** dogs. Many travel all over with their owners. They often ride in bags!

Chihuahuas can be **sassy**. They bark at strangers to keep their owners safe.

Chihuahuas like to cuddle.
They want to be near
their owners.

These small dogs have a
lot of love to give!

Glossary

alert—quick to notice or act

American Kennel Club—an organization that keeps track of dog breeds in the United States

breeds—types of dogs

coats—the hair or fur covering some animals

fawn—a light brown color

glossy—shiny and smooth

lean—thin

loyal—having constant support for someone

sassy—lively and bold

Techichis—an ancient breed of small dogs from Mexico

Toy Group—a group of the smallest dog breeds; most dogs in the Toy Group were bred to be companions.

To Learn More

AT THE LIBRARY

Graubart, Norman D. *My Dog*. New York, N.Y.: PowerKids Press, 2014.

Hengel, Katherine. *Chipper Chihuahuas*. Edina, Minn.: ABDO Pub., 2011.

Shores, Erika L. *All About Chihuahuas*. North Mankato, Minn.: Capstone Press, 2013.

ON THE WEB

Learning more about Chihuahuas is as easy as 1, 2, 3.

1. Go to www.factsurfer.com.

2. Enter "Chihuahuas" into the search box.

3. Click the "Surf" button and you will see a list of related web sites.

With factsurfer.com, finding more information is just a click away.

Index

The images in this book are reproduced through the courtesy of: Utekhina Anna, front cover; Eric Isselee, pp. 4, 12 (center, right), 15; holbox, p. 5; phloxii, p. 6; Cressida studio, p. 7; gvictoria, p. 8; Mark Raycroft/ Minden Pictures/ Corbis, p. 9; agoxa, p. 10; Pavel Hlystov, p. 11; Labat-Rouquette/ Kimball Stock, p. 12 (left); AnetaPics, p. 13; Leon Rafael, p. 14; Grisha Bruev, p. 17; Chiayiwangworks, p. 18; Annette Shaff, pp. 19, 21; Piti Tan, p. 20.